BUTTERFLIES

BY THE AUTHOR

BUTTERFLIES

By Dorothy Childs Hogner

Illustrated by Nils Hogner

THOMAS Y. CROWELL COMPANY

New York

We wish to thank Mr. John C. Pallister, Research Associate, Department of Entomology, of the American Museum of Natural History for his helpful suggestions on the butterfly manuscript. We also wish to thank Miss Alice Gray, M.A., Scientific Assistant at the Museum, for answering our questions on the anatomy and food habits of *Lepidoptera,* and Mr. Alfred R. Moulton, Inspector, Plant Pest Control Division, of the United States Department of Agriculture, for information on certain butterflies which pose a problem to agriculture.

CONTENTS

BUTTERFLIES

The Butterfly at Home

Where do you look for butterflies? The answer is easy. The second part of their name tells us. Butterflies fly about on their beautiful wings, so they are at home in the wide world of the air.

Some butterflies, like some birds, fly smoothly. Others flutter. Still others jerk along. They come down to feed or to rest. Although they may land with wings outspread, they usually rest with their wings held upward and together, over their back.

1

Look for butterflies in the daytime, for they like to go winging about when the sun shines.

You may see one light on the leaf of a tree, a flower, the stem of a plant, a blade of grass, or even on your window sill.

You will find butterflies where plants and trees grow, from the hot tropics to the cold Arctic. Butterflies and their young depend upon plants for their food.

What Is a Butterfly?

This may seem like a silly question, for everyone knows what a butterfly looks like. Not everyone knows what a butterfly really is. A butterfly has six legs, although the two front legs on some butterflies are so small that they are hard to see.

Now think of what other kinds of living creatures you have seen with six legs. Grasshoppers and crickets, of course, and flies, and bees, and beetles, and . . . well, you go on. The point is that butterflies and the many other different kinds of creatures with just six legs all belong to the same great class of animal life—the insects.

Some insects are wingless, but most of them, including butterflies, have two pairs of wings.

Most butterflies have slender bodies. Like the bodies of other insects, a butterfly's body is divided into three parts: the head, the middle or thorax, and the abdomen.

The Head

On the head of a butterfly are the antennae (the feelers), the eyes, and the mouth.

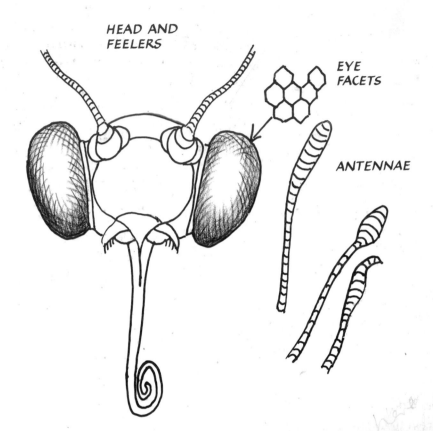

HEAD AND
FEELERS

EYE
FACETS

ANTENNAE

The feelers of most butterflies look alike. They
are long and slender. The tips are club-shaped.
Like you and me, a butterfly has two eyes, but
our eyes are quite small and simple. A butterfly's

eyes are big for its size. A butterfly's eyes are compound. This means that each eye is made up of hundreds of six-sided little eyes, all of which help a butterfly to see its way.

The butterfly's mouth has an upper lip and two short palps (also feelers).

The most important part of its mouth is the long tube through which it sucks up nectar, the sweet liquid of flowers. This is the favorite food of butterflies. When not in use, the sucking tube is coiled up like a spring.

A butterfly does not have a nose. The antennae of a butterfly act as both smeller and feeler. A butterfly may feel things by touching them with its antennae. The same feelers lead a butterfly to the fragrance of flowers and leaves and to other odors.

A butterfly hears with tiny hairlike organs on its body.

The Thorax or Middle

The thorax—the middle part of a butterfly's body—is divided into three parts, but these parts are so fitted together that you cannot see the divisions. You can best note their locations by looking for the legs and the wings. On each of these three sections of the thorax is one pair of legs, making a total of six legs. Each leg is made up of five jointed parts.

The front pair of wings is attached to the second part of the thorax. The hind wings are attached to the third part.

The wings themselves are, of course, very important to a butterfly. Veins are the framework of the wings. They give the wings their strength. Each group of butterflies has a different number or arrangement of wing veins.

WING VEINS

The wing veins have nothing to do with the beautiful colors and patterns on the wings. To see where the color lies, touch a butterfly's wings. What happens?

Off will come what appears to be dust, leaving the wing transparent. This "dust" is actually very fine, tiny flat scales, arranged like the scales of a fish. A butterfly's wings are covered with these scales. The scales give color to the wings, and make the butterflies very beautiful insects.

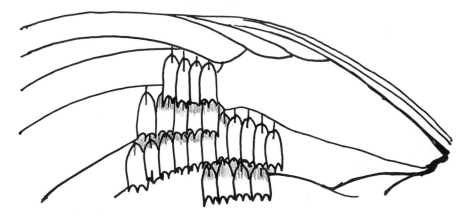

SCALES GREATLY MAGNIFIED

The body, the antennae, and the legs are also covered with scales. In fact, these scales are such an important part of a butterfly that scientists

have named the group of insects to which butterflies belong the scale-winged insects.

On either side of the last two sections of the
thorax are spiracles, the breathing holes. The butterfly takes in air through these holes.

The Abdomen

The third part of a butterfly's body, the abdomen, has nine parts or less. On either side are
more spiracles, or breathing holes. At the tip of
the abdomen are the external sex organs.

A Butterfly on the Inside

Breathing tubes take in air through the spiracles
and bring oxygen to the fluids of the body. Then

the air flows out, carrying with it the harmful carbon dioxide gas that has collected.

The heart of a butterfly is a long tube. This tube lies about where the backbone of a dog or cat lies. Butterflies, being insects, have no backbones nor, for that matter, any true bones. Their skeleton is made of chitin, a hard, hornlike material. Unlike our skeleton, which is under our skin, a butterfly's skeleton is on the outside.

Within the head of a butterfly are its brain and pharynx. The pharynx is a kind of pump. The front end of the pump is connected with the sucking tube. The back end is connected with the gullet. When the butterfly feeds, it uncoils its sucking tube and thrusts it into a flower. Then it pumps up the nectar (the sweet fluid in the flower) into the tube. From the tube the nectar goes on through the butterfly's gullet into its stomach.

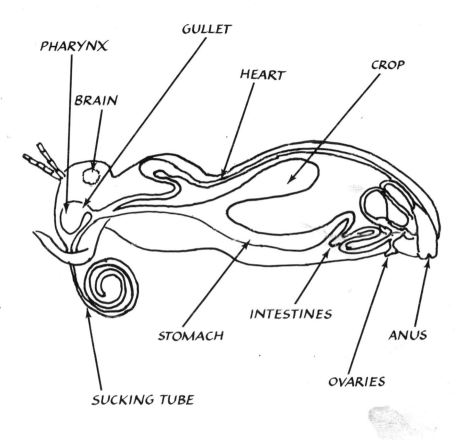

PHARYNX

GULLET

BRAIN

HEART

CROP

STOMACH

INTESTINES

ANUS

OVARIES

SUCKING TUBE

Juices may be stored temporarily in the crop, which is above the stomach. The nectar is digested in the stomach and the intestines. The wastes pass

11

out through the anus, the opening at the end of the abdomen.

Inside the end of the abdomen of a mother butterfly are the ovaries, where the eggs form.

A Butterfly's Box Lunch

What kind of flowers does a butterfly like best? Sit in the garden and watch.

You may see one land on a butterfly weed or a butterfly bush. Many people say that these are the *favorite* butterfly plants.

The butterfly weed is a showy kind of orange-flowered milkweed. The butterfly bush is a handsome shrub with lilac flowers.

As you will see for yourself, however, butterflies like to feed on the nectar of many different kinds of flowers. They seem to like best the

BUTTERFLY
BUSH

BUTTERFLY
WEED

flowers that are bright in color. They like splashy yellow, orange, and lilac blossoms. They also often feed on red or white blossoms, and on any flower that secretes nectar.

A Butterfly's Children

A mother butterfly lays her eggs singly, or by two and threes, or in clusters, on leaves of plants. She does not, however, lay her eggs on just any plant that she happens to alight upon. The young of different kinds of butterflies feed on only certain kinds of plants. Their life depends upon the mother's choosing one of the plants that they can eat.

Even though she could not eat a leaf if she tried (her mouth is not fitted for it), the mother picks out the right plants for her young. She does not do this by eyesight. She smells for the right plant with her feelers.

For example, a mother cabbage butterfly smells in a garden among the corn and potatoes until she finds a cabbage plant or another plant of the same family.

After laying her eggs, the mother butterfly flits away. She does not give her offspring another thought. She would not recognize one if she saw it. The creature that hatches out of a butterfly's egg, a tiny caterpillar, looks about as much like its mother as a snake looks like a turtle. It has a head and a long wormlike body made up of twelve rings. It has no wings but it has more legs than its parents.

Near the head of a caterpillar are three pairs of jointed legs. Behind are ten more legs. These ten legs are fleshy and, under a magnifying glass, look

somewhat like tiny elephants' legs. They usually have tiny hooks at the tip, called crochets. As might be expected in a creature with so many legs, a caterpillar's muscles are made for crawling.

To walk, a caterpillar starts by stretching forward the front three pairs of legs. Then it hitches forward the hindmost pair. Along come the in-between legs, two by two. The body moves forward in a crawling wave.

A Caterpillar Looks at the World

A caterpillar looks at the world through eyes different from its parents'. Instead of having a butterfly's compound eyes, it usually sees through six tiny simple eyes.

Instead of a long, graceful sucking tube for feeding, a caterpillar has fierce-looking jaws. Its mouth is made not for sucking but for chewing.

The feelers—and there are feelers—on a caterpillar's head are not long, like a butterfly's, but very, very short. The caterpillar seems to find its way with its palps (feelers), which are part of its under lip.

The caterpillar, however, breathes the same way as its parents do. It breathes through little spiracles (holes) in its sides.

A butterfly caterpillar has silk glands. Some caterpillars spin silk shelters for themselves.

A caterpillar does almost nothing all day and all night but eat and eat. It just grows and grows and grows.

Just as you and I get fatter when we eat a great deal, so does a caterpillar. You and I might even get too big for our jackets and "bust our buttons." A caterpillar gets too big for its skin; and, since it has no buttons, you might think it might be in a difficult position. Not so. A caterpillar's skin is made of the same horny materal, chitin, as the skin of a butterfly. Like the skin of a butterfly, it acts as a covering of the caterpillar's insides. When the skin gets too tight, it splits down the back. Then the caterpillar simply works its way out of its old jacket and crawls out in the new coat which has formed underneath. This is called molting.

Butterfly larvae (caterpillars) molt (shed their skins) from four to six times before they are fully grown.

How long does a larva remain a larva (or a caterpillar)? That depends upon the kind of butterfly and the climate. Some caterpillars may hibernate (sleep during the winter) as caterpillars, and in the spring turn into pupae and then into butterflies. In the United States, for most larvae the time as caterpillars is short. As soon as the caterpillar is ready to molt for the last time, the great change comes.

CATERPILLAR MOLTING

The Great Change

When a caterpillar is ready to change into a butterfly, it stops eating and lives off the fat of its body. After a day or two it fastens itself by its own silk to a twig or other object. The caterpillars of some butterflies fasten themselves by the tail end in a pad of silk. They hang head down.

Others make the same tail fastening but also spin a silk girdle around their middle. These butterflies may sit head up. They may hang with the head and body horizontal, under a twig. They do not hang upside down.

After the caterpillar has fastened itself in place, the old skin splits off for the last time. With this skin go all of the legs except the three front pairs.

These, the jointed legs, become the butterfly's legs. You can no longer see these legs, however. You can see only a kind of case. The case is called the pupa, or chrysalis.

Some pupae are spotted with silver or gold. Whether pretty or plain, the pupa looks lifeless. Nothing seems to be going on inside. Actually, a great deal is happening.

Wings are forming. The muscles are changing from crawling muscles into muscles used for flying. The mouth changes from a mouth that can chew solid food into one that can suck liquids out of flowers.

The ovaries, in which the eggs form in a mother butterfly, and the sex organs in a male butterfly become fully developed.

The compound eyes are formed.

Some kinds of caterpillars take only about ten

days to change into butterflies. These butterflies then creep out of their pupae at once. They spread their wings to dry. Then they fly away.

Most butterflies, however, rest during the winter as pupae, in the quiet state. They are not ready to come out and fly until spring.

How Do You Tell
One Butterfly from Another?

There are hundreds of different kinds of butterflies in the United States and Canada, including the Arctic Circle. To know them all takes years of study.

It is easy, however, to recognize the common butterflies. Just look at the shape and the color of their wings. Also, learn to know some caterpillars.

The Swallowtails

Members of this butterfly family are easy to recognize. As their name tells, most of them have tails on their hind wings. There are about twenty-five different kinds of swallowtails in North America, north of Mexico. They are all big, handsome butterflies.

The black swallowtail has black wings, with two rows of yellow spots. On the hind wings there are blue scales between the rows of yellow spots.

Watch for the black swallowtail in the vegetable garden. Here the mother black swallowtail goes to lay her eggs. She lays her eggs on the leaves of parsley and related plants, such as carrots and fennel. These are the plants on which the caterpillar of the black swallowtail feeds.

24

The caterpillar is called the parsley worm though, of course, it is not a true worm. When fully grown, it is a big, bright green caterpillar,

strikingly marked with black bands and yellow spots. Like a skunk, the parsley worm has scent glands. Touch one with a straw and see for yourself. It will raise two soft glands, up front, near its head. These glands give off a most unpleasant smell.

With a False Face

On Halloween you may put on a false face to fool people. The caterpillar of the tiger swallowtail is born with a false face.

The tiger swallowtail itself is a handsome butterfly. Its wings are usually bright yellow, with dark blue, black, and reddish markings. The mother tiger swallowtail may be mostly black.

Look for a larva of the tiger on the leaves of wild cherry, birch, poplar, or sassafras trees.

When small, this caterpillar is shiny, and black and white. As it grows, it turns mostly yellow and green. Its most striking markings are the two false eyes near the front. These false eyes are very big and look real. Like the parsley worm and the larvae of other swallowtail butterflies, the larva of the tiger swallowtail has scent glands. ·

TIGER SWALLOWTAIL AND FALSE FACE LARVA

When at rest, the caterpillar of the tiger swallowtail spins a little webbed hammock for itself
on top of a leaf.

28

Biggest Butterfly

The biggest swallowtail, the giant swallowtail, has a wingspan of up to five and a half inches. This makes it the very biggest of all our butterflies.

The giant swallowtail is dark colored, with many large yellow spots. It is common in the south, where the caterpillar is called the orange dog. The caterpillar feeds on the leaves of orange, lemon, and grapefruit trees. In the north it feeds on the prickly ash.

Many beautiful swallowtails live in the tropics. They look quite different from ours. The *coon*

COON COON SWALLOWTAIL

coon swallowtail of the island of Java has very narrow, long, black-and-yellow hind wings. It looks like a big, fancy letter X.

Butterflies with Yellow, White, or Orange-Tipped Wings

The sulphurs (the yellows), the whites, and the orange-tips are a large family of common butterflies. They are named after the color of their wings. The wings of the sulphurs are yellow or orange. The whites, of course, have white wings. The orange-tips have white wings, too, but the wings of the orange-tips are greenish underneath and they usually have orange tips on their front wings.

All three—the sulphurs, the whites, and the

orange-tips—have darker markings on the edges of their wings.

Most butterflies of this family are small to medium in size.

The Roadside or Puddle Butterfly

The roadside butterfly, one of the yellows, is often seen flitting along a roadside or flying around a swampy pool. Its yellow wings have black markings.

It is sometimes called the clouded sulphur.

The caterpillar of the roadside butterfly feeds on clover.

The dog's-head butterfly, another of the yellows, has lemon-yellow wings, marked with black. It is called the dog's-head because the yel-

ROADSIDE
BUTTERFLY

DOG'S-
HEAD

low shape on each front wing looks something
like the head of a dog.

The caterpillar of the dog's-head butterfly also
feeds on clover.

33

Most Harmful Butterfly

Nearly everyone knows by sight the most harmful butterfly. It is the cabbage butterfly, one of the whites.

The cabbage butterfly has black markings on the edges of its dull-white wings. The under wings are mostly pale lemon-yellow, and sometimes the upper wings, too, are tinged with yellow.

The cabbage butterfly is not native to America. It came here as an immigrant from Europe, probably as a stowaway in a load of cabbage, on a ship. It arrived in Quebec, Canada, about a hundred years ago. Since then, its great-great-many-times-great-grandchildren have found their way into everyone's cabbage patch. It is now one of our most common butterflies, both north and south, from the Atlantic to the Pacific oceans.

CABBAGE BUTTERFLY

The cabbage butterfly itself, of course, does no harm. Like other butterflies, it flits about, looking pretty in the sunshine. It is the caterpillars of the cabbage butterfly that do damage in the garden.

The mother butterfly lays her eggs, one by one, on the leaves of a cabbage or some other member of this plant family, such as a radish or a turnip plant. She lays just a few eggs on each leaf.

The caterpillars that hatch from these eggs are bright green marked with lemon-yellow. First, they eat up their own egg shells. Then off they go, chewing up cabbage leaves at a greedy rate.

Farmers and gardeners must spend money and time on sprays to kill these hungry caterpillars which would otherwise ruin the crops.

Butterflies with Blue, Copper, and Hair-Streaked Wings

The blues, the coppers, and the hair-streaks belong to a family of small delicate-winged butterflies. Most of them have a wingspread of an inch or a little more. The blues and the coppers are named after the color of their wings. The upper surface of the wings of the blues is usually blue.

HAIR-STREAK

The coppers have brown or orange-red wings with black markings and an over-all copper tinge.

The hair-streaks take their name from the narrow hairlike streaks that mark their under wings. The upper surface of the wings of most hair-streaks is dark in color, but a few have bright green or blue markings.

The caterpillars of this family look more like slugs than caterpillars.

Honey for the Ants

Most of the blues are found only in the west. The spring azure, the common blue, is at home over most of the United States. This delicate little butterfly is seen flitting about early in the spring. It also may be seen all summer long.

Its upper wings are blue with a violet tinge. The under wings are light ash-gray in color, marked with tiny dark dots.

SPRING AZURE

The caterpillar of this common little blue butterfly feeds on the buds and flowers of dogwood, snake root, and other plants.

It has something that most caterpillars do not. On the tenth and eleventh sections of the caterpillar of the common blue butterfly there are honey tubes. Ants often watch over these caterpillars. They look upon them as their honey pot. They like to sip the sweet liquid from the caterpillars' honey tubes.

The Very Littlest Butterfly

The very smallest butterfly in all of North America is the pygmy blue. It has a wingspread of only about three fifths of an inch.

It is one of the blues because of its form and

wing structure. Its wings are not blue, but brown with white spots and a white fringe on the front wings. Dark spots, circled by shining scales, mark the edge of the under wings.

The pygmy is at home in the states of Florida, Alabama, Mississippi, Louisiana, and Texas.

The American Copper

The American copper is common in California, Washington, Oregon, and Canada. It is also at

AMERICAN COPPER

home in the states bordering Canada, and in the Northeast, south along the Appalachian Mountains into Georgia.

The front wings of the American copper are orange-red marked with black spots, and a black band on the edge. The hind wings are copper-brown. A wide orange-red band dotted with four black dots is on the wing edge.

The larva feeds on dock and sorrel.

The Odd Children
of the Wanderer

The wanderer, or the harvester, is a little brown butterfly, with a wingspread of about an inch. It belongs to the same family as the blues, the coppers, and the hair-streaks. No one knows why it is called the wanderer. It does not wander far. It is not very common.

The wanderer is interesting because of the unusual habits of its caterpillars. The caterpillars of

THE WANDERER

most butterflies feed on plants. The children of the wanderer eat meat.

The caterpillars of the wanderer feed on aphids. These are tiny, white, woolly insects. The aphids, in turn, feed on alder leaves. So, look for the wanderer and its children where alders grow—from northern Florida to the state of Maine, and westward into Kansas.

Four-Footed Butterflies

There are several families of butterflies that use only four of their six feet for walking. This is because the front pair of legs of these butterflies is too small and short.

Among these are the big, handsome milkweed butterflies. The family is so named because their caterpillars feed on milkweed.

Southward Bound

The commonest member of the four-footed milkweed butterfly family is the monarch. The monarch is a beautiful, big butterfly, with a wing-spread up to three and one half inches. The wings are light brown with black veins and edgings. There are two rows of white spots on the outer wing edges.

No doubt you have seen many monarchs. They are the strongest fliers among the butterflies. They really get about. They are at home almost everywhere in North and South America. They are also seen on other continents.

In the North of our country in the fall the monarchs gather in great flocks numbering a thousand or more. They fly south together for the winter. On their way they come down to rest on trees to which they can cling. Maples, willows, oaks, and pines are among the best. Some monarchs go off to rest by themselves or in small groups. Others crowd together in the same tree.

You might think that a flock of birds, also flying south, would gobble up a flock of monarchs before the butterflies had flown far. Not so. A little black patch on the upper surface of each hind wing of the father monarch gives off a smell that

MONARCHS
RESTING

birds find disagreeable. So the birds leave the monarchs alone.

In the spring, some of the monarchs begin to fly north again, laying their eggs singly on the leaves of the milkweed plants.

The full-grown monarch caterpillar is greenish yellow in color, with black bands. It changes into a butterfly in a chrysalis (pupa) that is mostly green, marked with spots of gold.

Brush-Footed Butterflies

The brush-footed butterflies are another family of four-footed butterflies. They are called brush-footed because the feet on the front pair of legs look like little brushes. Like the monarch, their front legs are so short that they are useless for walking.

The brush-footed butterflies are the largest family of all the butterfly families. They are found nearly all over the world, from the high mountains to the low valleys, from the far north to the hot tropics.

They are medium to big in size.

One of the brush-footed butterflies, the viceroy, is a mimic. It looks so much like a monarch that it fools even the birds. The birds know that the monarchs smell too bad to eat; and, when they see a viceroy, they leave it alone, too. This is fortunate because the viceroy does *not* have a wing patch that gives off a disagreeable odor, as the monarch has.

You can easily tell a viceroy from a monarch by its slightly smaller size and its markings. The viceroy has only one row of white spots on the outer edge of its wings, while the monarch has two rows. The viceroy also has a black band across its hind wings.

Red Admiral

A handsome member of the brush-footed butterfly family, the red admiral, is a common butterfly over nearly all of North America and Europe. The red admiral has purplish black wings marked with white spots and broad stripes. These stripes are red on the under wings and orange on the upper wings. It has a wingspread of from two to three inches. The edges of the wings are notched.

The caterpillar of the red admiral feeds on nettles.

The red admiral may spend the winter in its pupa. Then the butterfly comes out in the spring. Or the red admiral may come out of its pupa as

soon as it has changed from a caterpillar into a butterfly. Then the butterfly itself hibernates (sleeps) until spring as a butterfly. This is not common among butterflies.

Painted Beauty

Another pretty brush-footed butterfly, the painted beauty, looks much like the red admiral. It is about the same size. Its markings are different. The brown and blackish wings are splashed with reddish orange. There are white spots on the upper surface of the front pair. There are two large eyespots on the under surface of each hind wing.

The caterpillar of the painted beauty feeds on everlasting plants.

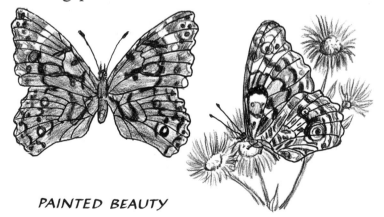

PAINTED BEAUTY

Great Spangled Fritillary

Other common members of the brush-footed butterfly family are the fritillaries—the silver-spots. They are easy to identify. The under wings of most of them have conspicuous silver spots. The main wing color is brown, marked with the silver spots and many dots and wriggly lines.

Some of the silver-spots are quite small. Others are quite big. Among the biggest is the great spangled fritillary. It has a wingspan of up to four inches.

The caterpillars of the silver-spots feed at night on violets.

Mourning Cloak

The mourning cloak is a purplish brown butterfly. There is a broad yellow band, dotted with brown, on the edge of its wings. There is also a row of blue spots next to the yellow band. It has a wingspan of three and a half inches.

The mourning cloak is a common butterfly, from the southern border of the United States to the Arctic Circle. It is one of the few butterflies that winters as a butterfly. Therefore, this butter-fly is often seen flying early in the spring.

The caterpillar of the mourning cloak feeds mostly on poplar, elm, and willow trees.

MOURNING CLOAK

Wood Nymph

The common wood nymph belongs to a third family of four-footed butterflies. This medium-sized brown butterfly is easy to identify. Look for a wide yellow band across each front wing. Each band is marked with two black and white eyespots. There is also one eyespot on each hind wing.

The Arctic butterflies belong to the same four-footed butterfly family as the wood nymph. To see one you must travel to the Arctic, or climb to high mountain tops in the United States.

These Arctic butterflies are the great-great-many-times-great-grandchildren of butterflies that lived during the Ice Age. They cannot stand hot weather.

One, the White Mountain butterfly, now lives on the chilly peaks of the White Mountains in

New Hampshire, and the Rocky Mountains, in Colorado. It is a brown butterfly, with a wingspan of about one and three quarters inches.

The Skippers

You can tell a skipper by the odd way in which it flies. It makes sudden, quick movements and seems to skip through the air.

You can sometimes tell skippers by the way they rest. Some hold their front wings upright over the body, as common butterflies usually do. Others spread their wings out flat, like some moths.

Most of the skippers are small butterflies, but their bodies are stout, more like a moth's body than a butterfly's.

When the skipper caterpillars are ready to

change into butterflies, they make a silk covering
that is almost like a moth's cocoon.

The pretty silver-spotted skipper is dark brown
with yellow spots on its front wings and one large
silver spot on the under side of each hind wing.

58

The caterpillar makes a leaf into a tent by fastening it together with a silk thread.

Some Cousins

A butterfly has several thousand cousins living in the United States and Canada. These are the moths.

Look for moths after dark. When a moth comes to rest, it spreads its wings out flat or folds them *down* over the body. A butterfly usually folds its wings *up* over its back.

CODDLING
MOTH

In many ways a moth looks very much like a butterfly. Most moths, however, have stouter bodies. And the antennae are different. Remember that a butterfly's feelers have clublike tips. The feelers of most moths are threadlike or featherlike.

Why Not Rear a Caterpillar?

It is interesting to watch a caterpillar turn into a pupa.

Unless you know a great many caterpillars, one from the other, how will you know what kind you've got? To make sure, start with a parsley worm. You are certain to find one in the parsley bed before summer is over.

A rearing cage may be made of a standard aquarium, 14 by 10 by 8 inches—without water, of course. Set a bowl of water in the cage. Put the stems of a few sprigs of parsley in the bowl, with the leaves hanging over the edge. Then place a cover over the bowl so that the caterpillar will not fall in and drown. Weight the cover down with a small stone to keep the parsley stems in the water. Place a screen over the top of the aquarium.

Now put the parsley worm in your cage.

To keep your parsley worm happy, you need only give it more parsley after it has eaten the first bunch. Remember that a parsley worm in the garden is used to dew and rain. So, every second day or so, sprinkle it *very* lightly with water.

Suppose your parsley worm is an inch long when you find it. It will be full-grown and ready to change into a pupa in about nine days. In any case, it will tell you when it is ready. Watch for these signs.

It will stop eating and will wander restlessly about. As likely as not, before night comes, it will choose a place to rest, probably near the top of its cage. Slowly its body will grow shorter and thicker.

Next day it will cling to this spot, head up, tail down, all day long. Before this second day has ended, it will fasten its hind end to the cage with a tiny tuft of silk. Then it will spin out a fine silk girdle around its middle to hold itself, more or less, head up.

Some time on the third day, it will become a pupa. To be sure that you do not miss seeing this happen, watch constantly for signs of wriggling. The minute the caterpillar begins to wriggle, stay by the cage. In a few moments the caterpillar will twist every ring of its body violently. Suddenly the skin over its head will turn pale in color and become all crinkly. Then the crinkly skin will split in a V.

Wriggle, wriggle. The wriggles continue. As you might slip off a pair of tights, the caterpillar slowly wriggles out of its old skin. In a few more seconds the old skin falls off the caterpillar's hind end onto the floor of the cage. The old skin looks like a tiny, rumpled, worn-out sock.

What remains is a greenish case—the pupa. After a few more wriggles, the pupa sits still. Hours pass. The pupa turns ash-gray and brown in color. It is lifeless-looking.

To keep your parsley worm pupa over winter and see the black swallowtail butterfly come out, remember that you must not let the pupa get too dry. If it were out of doors, it would get rained on. You must make it rain in the cage. To do this, simply sprinkle the pupa lightly with water now and then. Sprinkle it no more than once a week.

In the wilds, a black swallowtail butterfly comes out of its pupa in the spring. Chances are that if you keep yours indoors, it may come out earlier. So keep watch over your cage. When the butterfly does come out, its wings will be folded. Slowly it will stretch them out to dry. Then it will take off, into the air.

Rear a parsley worm in your own house, or go out and watch caterpillars in their natural home in the garden, in the fields, and in the woods. Or merely sit in the sun and watch the butterflies themselves go winging by in the air or coming down to sip the sweet nectar of bright flowers.

Whichever you may do, we are sure that you will find butterflies beautiful and interesting insects.

INDEX

About the Author
and Illustrator

Dorothy Childs Hogner is a Connecticut Yankee born in Manhattan. She spent her first year in New York and then the Childs family moved to an old white clapboard house on a hundred-acre farm in Connecticut.

Mrs. Hogner attended Wellesley College, Parsons Art School in New York, and was graduated from the University of New Mexico. She is the author of many books for children, several of which are illustrated by her husband, Nils Hogner.

Mr. Hogner, who is primarily a mural painter, is an active member of the National Society of Mural Painters and the Architectural League of New York. His "Memorial to the Four Chaplains" may be seen at Temple University in Philadelphia.

The Hogners spend some time in their New York City apartment; but they are usually found at their herb farm in Litchfield, Connecticut, where they raise everything from basil to sweet cicely.